IMPERFECT THIRST

ALSO BY GALWAY KINNELL

POETRY

What a Kingdom It Was   *1960*

Flower Herding on Mount Monadnock   *1964*

Body Rags   *1968*

First Poems 1946–1954   *1971*

The Book of Nightmares   *1971*

The Avenue Bearing the Initial of Christ into
the New World: Poems 1946–64   *1974*

Mortal Acts, Mortal Words   *1980*

Selected Poems   *1982*

The Past   *1985*

When One Has Lived a Long Time Alone   *1990*

Three Books   *1993*

PROSE

Black Light   *1966*

Walking Down the Stairs: Selections from Interviews   *1978*

How the Alligator Missed Breakfast (for children)   *1982*

TRANSLATIONS

Bitter Victory (novel by René Hardy)   *1956*

The Poems of François Villon   *1965*

On the Motion and Immobility of Douve
(poems by Yves Bonnefoy)   *1968*

Lackawanna Elegy (poems by Yvan Goll)   *1970*

The Poems of François Villon (second version)   *1977*

EDITION

The Essential Whitman   *1987*

GALWAY KINNELL

Imperfect
Thirst

Houghton Mifflin Company

BOSTON   NEW YORK

1994

For information about permission to reproduce selections from this book, write to Permissions, Houghton Mifflin Company, 215 Park Avenue South, New York, New York 10003.

Library of Congress Cataloging-in-Publication Data

Kinnell, Galway, date.
 Imperfect thirst / Galway Kinnell.
  p. cm.
  ISBN 0-395-71089-8
  I. Title.
 PS3521.I582I46 1994
 811'.54 — dc20   94-27044   CIP

Book design by Anne Chalmers

Printed in the United States of America

STN 10 9 8 7 6 5 4 3 2 1

Some of the poems in this book originally appeared in the following publications:
The American Poetry Review: The Deconstruction of Emily Dickinson, My
         Mother's R & R, The Night, The Pen, Showing My Father
         Through Freedom, The Striped Snake and the Goldfinch.
Antaeus: "The Music of Poetry."
The Atlantic Monthly: The Cellist.
The Paris Review: Lackawanna.
Ploughshares: Sheffield Ghazals (The Biting Insects, Paradise Elsewhere,
         Collusion of Elements, Driving West, Passing the Cemetery)
         under the title Sheffield Pastorals.
Poetry: Neverland.
Princeton University Library Chronicle: The Road Across Skye.
The New Yorker: Flies, Hitchhiker, The Man in the Chair, Parkinson's
         Disease, Picnic, Rapture.
The Threepenny Review: Running on Silk.

TO BOBBIE

If your eyes are not deceived by the mirage
Do not be proud of the sharpness of your understanding;
It may be your freedom from this optical illusion
Is due to the imperfectness of your thirst.

—Sohrawardi

CONTENTS

PROEM

The Pen   3

I

My Mother's R & R   9
Showing My Father Through Freedom   10
Hitchhiker   12
The Man in the Chair   13
Picnic   15

II

The Cellist   19
Running on Silk   21
The Deconstruction of Emily Dickinson   23
The Night   26
Trees   28

III

SHEFFIELD GHAZALS

The Biting Insects   35
Paradise Elsewhere   36
Collusion of Elements   37
Driving West   38
Passing the Cemetery   39

IV

Parkinson's Disease   43
Telephoning in Mexican Sunlight   46

"The Music of Poetry" 48

Rapture 50

The Road Across Skye 52

v

Lackawanna 57

Holy Shit 61

Flies 68

The Striped Snake and the Goldfinch 74

Neverland 79

PROEM

THE PEN

Its work is memory.

It engraves sounds into paper and fills them with pounded nutgall.

It can transcribe most of the sounds that the child, waking early, not
       yet knowing which language she will one day speak, sings.

Asleep in someone's pocket in an airplane, the pen dreams of paper,
       and a feeling of pressure comes into it, and, like a boy
       dreaming of Grace Hamilton, who sits in front of him in
       the fifth grade, it could spout.

An old pen with unresilient ink sac may make many scratches before
       it inks.

The pen's alternation of lifts and strokes helps thoughts to keep
       coming in a rhythmic flow.

When several thoughts arrive together, the pen may resort to
       scribbling "blah blah," meaning, come back to this later.

Much of what pens write stands for "blah blah."

In the Roman system, the pen moves to the right, and at the margin
       swerves backward and downward—perhaps dangerous
       directions, but necessary for reentering the past.

The pen is then like the person who gets out of the truck, goes
       around to the rear, signals to the driver, and calls, "C'mon
       back."

Under increased concentration the pen spreads its nib, thickening the
       words that attempt to speak the unspeakable.

These are the fallen-angel words.

Ink is their ichor.

They have a mineral glint, given by clarity of knowing, even in hell.

The pen also uses ink to obfuscate, like the cuttlefish, by inculcating
       the notions that reality happens one complete sentence after

another, and that if we have words for an event, we understand
it—as in:

> How's your pa?
> He died.
> Oh.

When my father died, leaving my mother and me alone in the house,
    I don't know even now what happened.

What did Rilke understand on the death of his father, who by then
    had become a speck in the distance?

Did his mother suddenly become larger?

It seems that soon after she married him, Rilke's wife also began
    turning into a speck.

He told her in eloquent letters it was good for his artistic development
    for them to live apart; meanwhile women arrived from all over
    Europe, to spend their allotment of nights in his bed.

I called it "my work" when I would spend weeks on the road, often in
    the beds of others.

This Ideal pen, with vulcanite body, can't resist dredging up the
    waywardness of my youth.

Fortunately pens run out of ink.

Villon had to cut short the bitter bequests of *Le Lais* when his inkwell
    froze and his candle blew out.

Like a camel at an oasis with stomachs completely empty, the pen
    thrusts itself into the ink and suctions in near-silence.

Filled, it starts again laying trudge marks across the paper.

Yesterday, when trying to write about my sister Wendy, my little
    mother in childhood, I couldn't find the words in the ink.

Then I had a visit from a poet a few years widowed, who talked about
    her husband and how she felt thwarted in her writing and

had lost her way—though in the rhythmical tumbling forth of her words she seemed to be finding it.

I wished I had collected some of the mascara-blackened fluid on her cheeks to mix into my ink.

But when I started writing about Wendy again, the ink had replenished its vocabulary, and from the street came the bleats of a truck in reverse gear and a cry, "C'mon back, c'mon back."

I

MY MOTHER'S R & R

She lay late in bed. Maybe she was sick,
though she was never sick. There were
pink flowers in full blossom in the wallpaper
and motes like bits of something ground up
churning in sun rays from the windows.
We climbed into bed with her.
Perhaps she needed comforting,
and she was alone, and she let us take
a breast each out of the loose slip.
"Let's make believe we're babies,"
Derry said. We put the large pink
flowers at the end of those lax breasts
into our mouths and sucked with enthusiasm.
She laughed and seemed to enjoy our play.
Perhaps intoxicated by our pleasure,
or frustrated by the failure of the milk
to flow, we sucked harder, probably
our bodies writhed, our eyes flared,
maybe she could feel our teeth.
Abruptly she took back her breasts
and sent us from the bed, two small
hungry boys enflamed and driven off
by the she-wolf. But we had got our nip,
and in the empire we would found,
we would taste every woman and expel
each one who came to resemble her.

SHOWING MY FATHER THROUGH FREEDOM

His steps rang in the end room
of the henhouse of ten rooms in a row
someone had lent my father as a place
to put the family for the summer
while he stayed behind doing his odd jobs.
This would be his one visit, and I ran
through the dark of the empty rooms
until he bent down out of the gloom like a god
and picked me up and carried me back into the lamplight.
The next day my mother and I showed him through Freedom.
The strawberry ice cream in the Harmony Tea Shop,
which my mother called the Patisserie, was pink
with red bruises. Lettie the postmistress
said, with her sweet regretfulness, perhaps acquired
from palping whatever billets-doux passed
in or out of Freedom, as she said nearly every day
to one or another of us children, "Nothing today, dear."
John, who pumped gas probably no more
than a dozen times a day, sat back in his chair
under the sign of Pegasus. I ran to him,
to get on the knee where he put me
whenever my mother and I came by, happy
that my father would see this full-grown
man was my friend, and would respect me.
But after he greeted us, John turned and, when he sat again,
leaned forward and put his elbows on his knees.
The three of them conversed. My father did his best.
"Yes, it *has* been," of the wet summer.
"They *are* sudden," of the lightning storms.

I lingered at the knee. My sitting on it,
and my mother and John talking while I sat,
was that a secret? Suddenly I was like
somebody propped up in a hospital bed,
who can see, hear, almost understand,
and is unable to speak.

HITCHHIKER

After a moment, the driver, a salesman
for Travelers Insurance heading for
Topeka, said, "What was that?"
I, in my Navy uniform, still useful
for hitchhiking though the war was over,
said, "I think you hit somebody."
I knew he had. The round face, opening
in surprise as the man bounced off the fender,
had given me a look as he swept past.
"Why didn't you say something?" The salesman
stepped hard on the brakes. "I thought you saw,"
I said. I didn't know why. It came to me
I could have sat next to this man all the way
to Topeka without saying a word about it.
He opened the car door and looked back.
I did the same. At the roadside,
in the glow of a streetlight, was a body.
A man was bending over it. For an instant
it was myself, in a time to come,
bending over the body of my father.
The man stood and shouted at us, "Forget it!
He gets hit all the time!" Oh.
A bum. We were happy to forget it.
The rest of the way, into dawn in Kansas,
when the salesman dropped me off, we did not speak,
except, as I got out, I said, "Thanks,"
and he said, "Don't mention it."

THE MAN IN THE CHAIR

I glanced in as I walked past
the door of the room where he sat
in the easy chair with the soiled area
along the top from the olive oil.
I think I noticed something—
a rigidity in the torso, making it
unable to settle into the cushions,
or a slackness in the neck,
causing the head to tilt forward,
or a shaking in the lifted right fist,
as though he were pushing a hammer
handle back with all his force, to pull
a spike driven nineteen years before
the end of the nineteenth century
into lignum vitae so dense the steel
must have cried out in excruciated singsong,
or an acute angle in the knees,
as if he held his feet inches off
the floor to keep them from the whitish
wash of mist risen from some freshly
dug pit simmering across it,
or the jerk of a leg, as if a hand
just then reached through the floor
and tried to grab it. I think I noticed,
yet I did not stop, or go in, or speak.
For his part he could not have spoken,
that day, or any day, for he had a human
version of the pip, the disease that thickens birds'
vocal cords and throttles their song.

I had it too, probably caught from him,
and I could not speak my feelings except
to the beings I had invented far within.
I walked past, into my room, shut
the door, and sat down at my desk,
where I had spent many hours
passing one number through another and
drawing the little row of survivors on top,
while my mother sat across from me
watching for mistakes upside down.
I wrote, and as I did I allowed
to be audible in the room only
the scritches of the pen nib, a sound
like a rat crawling around in the dark
interior of a wall, making a nest of shreds.
All other sounds, including
the words I never said to him,
the cries to him I did not make, I forced down
through the paper, the desk, the floor,
the surface of the earth, the roof
of that dismal region where they stood,
two or three of them who had reached up
and had him by the foot, and were pulling hard.

PICNIC

When my father was three years dead and dying
away more quickly than other dead fathers do,
I took my mother in my 1935 green Ford
for a picnic on the Back Shore of Cape Cod,
where Henry Beston had gone alone
and chronicled a year spent attempting to feel
kinship with the elements and the beach creatures,
who demanded nothing and did not expect to be loved.
I swam, not far out; I have always felt fear
when swimming on top of very deep water.
When I came back I sat next to my mother on the towel,
and we ate the lunch she had wrapped in the same
Cut-rite wax paper she had wrapped my sandwiches in
in J. C. Potter School, paraffined to the degree
of cloudy translucency that indicated the extent
we saw, and the extent we did not see,
ourselves as two who had done nothing
to avert the explosion in my father's chest.
As I rubbed myself with sun oil, concentrating
in the way I concentrated on anything that
did not entail knowing what it meant
for me to be a son of him or her, she said, "Oh,
you have hair on your legs, I never thought you did."

II

THE CELLIST

At intermission I find her backstage
still practicing the piece coming up next.
She calls it the "solo in high dreary."
Her bow niggles at the string like a hand
stroking skin it never wanted to touch.
Probably under her scorn she is sick
that she can't do better by it. As I am,
by the dreary in me, such as the disparity
between all the tenderness I've received
and the amount I've given, and the way
I used to shrug off the imbalance
simply as how things are, as if the male
were constituted like those coffeemakers
that produce less black bitter than the quantity
of sweet clear you pour in — forgetting about
how much I spilled through unsteady walking,
and that lot I flung on the ground
in suspicion, and for fear I wasn't worthy,
and all I threw out for reasons I don't understand yet.
"Break a leg!" somebody tells her.
Back in my seat, I can see she is nervous
when she comes out; her hand shakes as she
re-dog-ears the top corners of the big pages
that look about to flop over on their own.
Now she raises the bow — its flat bundle of hair
harvested from the rear ends of horses — like a whetted
scimitar she is about to draw across a throat,
and attacks. In a back alley a cat opens
its pink-ceilinged mouth, gets netted

in full yowl, clubbed, bagged, bicycled off, haggled open,
gutted, the gut squeezed down to its highest pitch,
washed, then sliced into cello strings that bring
a screaming into this duet of hair and gut.
Now she is flying—tossing back the goblets
of Saint-Amour standing empty,
half-empty, or full on the tablecloth-
like sheet music. Her knees tighten
and loosen around the big-hipped creature
wailing and groaning between them
as if locked with her in syzygial amplexus.
The music seems to rise from the crater left
when heaven was torn up and taken off the earth;
more likely it comes up through her priest's dress,
up from that clump of hair which by now
may be so wet with its waters, miraculous as the waters
the fishes multiplied in at Galilee, that
each hair wicks a portion all the way out
to its tip and fattens a droplet on the bush
of half notes now glittering in that dark.
At last she lifts off the bow and sits back.
Her face shines with the unselfconsciousness of a cat
screaming at night and the teary radiance of one
who gives everything no matter what has been given.

RUNNING ON SILK

A man in the black twill and gold braid of a pilot
and a woman with the virginal alertness
flight attendants had in the heyday
of stewardesses go running past
as if they have hopped off one plane
and are running to hop on another.
They look to me absolutely like lovers;
in the verve and fleetness of their sprint
you can see them running toward each other
inside themselves. The man pulls a luggage
cart with one suitcase bungeed on top of another,
and the woman...my God, she holds her
high heels in her hand and runs on silk!
I see us, as if preserved in the amber
of forty-year-old Tennessee sour-mash whiskey
poured over cherishing ice, put down
our glasses, sidestep through groups
and pairs gruffing and tinkling
to each other, go out the door,
hoof and click down two flights of stairs.
Maybe he wonders what goes on with his wife
and that unattached young man he left
her laughing with—and finds them not
where he left them, not in the kitchen,
not anywhere, and goes out to the hall and
hears laughter jangling in the stairwell
cut off by the bang of the outside door. In the street
she pulls off her shoes and runs on stocking feet
—laughing and crying *taxiii! taxiii!*

as if we were ecstatic worshipers springing
down a beach in Bora-Bora — toward a cab
suffusing its back end in red brake light.
As I push her in, a voice behind us calls
bop! bop! like a stun gun, or a pet name.
Out the taxi's rear window I glimpse him,
stopped dead, one foot on the sidewalk,
one in the gutter, a hand on his heart. *Go! go!*
we cry to the driver. After we come together,
to our surprise, for we are strangers,
my telephone also starts making a lot
of anxious, warbling, weeping-like noises.
I put it on the floor, with a pillow on it,
and we lie back and listen with satisfaction
to the rings as if they were dumdum bullets,
meant for us, spending their force in feathers.
A heavy man trotting by knocks my leg with his bag
but doesn't seem to notice and trots on.
Could he be running after those two high-flyers
who have run out of sight? Will I find him, up ahead,
stopped at a closed departure gate, like that man
that night forty years ago, as if turned to wood
and put out by his murderers to sell cigars?

THE DECONSTRUCTION OF EMILY DICKINSON

The lecture had ended when I came in,
and the professor was answering questions.
I do not know what he had been doing with her
poetry, but now he was speaking of her
as a victim of reluctant male publishers.
When the questions dwindled, I put up my hand.
I said the ignorant meddling of the Springfield *Daily Republican*
and the hidebound response of literary men,
and the gulf between the poetic wishfulness
then admired and her own harsh knowledge,
had let her see that her poems
would not be understood in her time;
and therefore, passionate to publish,
she vowed not to publish again. I said
I would recite a version of her vow,

> Publication – is the Auction
> Of the Mind of Man –

but before I could, the professor broke in.
"Yes," he said, "'the Auction'—'auction,' from *augere, auctum*, to
　　augment, to author…"
"Let's hear the poem!" "The poem!" several women,
who at such a moment are more outspoken than men, shouted,
but I kept still and he kept going.
"In *auctum* the economy of the signifier is split, revealing an uncon-
　　scious collusion in the bourgeois commodification of con-
　　sciousness. While our author says 'no,' the unreified text says
　　'yes,' yes?"
He kissed his lips together and turned to me

saying, "Now, may we hear the poem?"
I waited a moment for full effect.
Without rising to my feet, I said,
"Professor, to understand Dickinson
it may not always be necessary to uproot her words.
Why not, first, try *listening* to her?
Loyalty forbids me to recite her poem now."
No, I didn't say that—I realized
she would want me to finish him off with one wallop.
So I said, "Professor, I thought you
would welcome the words of your author.
I see you prefer to hear yourself speak."
No, I held back—for I could hear her
urging me to put outrage into my voice
and substance into my argument.
I stood up so that everyone might see
the derision in my smile. "Professor," I said,
"you live in Amherst at the end of the twentieth century.
For you 'auction' means a quaint event
where somebody coaxes out the bids
on butter churns on a summer Saturday.
Forget etymology, this is history.
In Amherst in 1860 'auction' meant
the slave auction, you dope!"
Well, I didn't say that either,
although I have said them all,
many times, in the middle of the night.
In reality, I stood up and recited the poem
like a schoolboy called upon in class.

My voice gradually weakened, and the women
who had called out for the poem
now looked as though they were thinking
of errands to be done on the way home.
When I finished, the professor smiled.
"Thank you. So, what at first some of us may have taken as a simple
        outcry, we all now see is an ambivalent, self-subversive text."
As people got up to go, I moved
into that sanctum within me where Emily
sometimes speaks a verse, and listened
for a sign of how she felt, such as,
"Thanks – Sweet – countryman –
for wanting – to Sing out – of Me –
after all that Humbug." But she was silent.

THE NIGHT

Just as paint seems to leap from the paintbrush
to clapboards that have gone many years unpainted
and disappear into them almost with a slurp,
so their words, as they lie and talk, their faces
almost touching, jump from one mouth to the other
without apparent sound except little lip-wetting smacks.
When their mouths touch at last they linger, making
small eating motions and suction squeaks.
She licks three slithery syllables on his chest,
looks up, smiles, shines him the same three.
In his gasps suspense and gratefulness mix,
as in the crinkling unwrapping of Christmas packages.
Where he touches her she glisses smooth and shining
as the lower lip of a baby tantalizing its gruel bowl
with lengthening and shortening dangles of drool.
Her moans come with a slight delay, as if the sequence
happens across a valley, the touch and then the cry.
Their bones almost hit—the purpose of flesh
may be to keep the skeletons from bruising each other.
One of them calls out in cackling, chaotic rattles,
like a straw suddenly sucking the bottom. Then, with a sound
like last bathwater seized by the Coriolis force,
the other calls out. They lie holding each other.
For a moment the glue joining body and soul does not ache.
They are here and not here, like the zebra,
whose flesh has been sliced up and reassembled
in alternating layers with matter from elsewhere.
The sense that each one had of being divided in two
has given way to the knowledge that each is half

of the whole limb-tangle appearing like a large
altricial hatchling occupying much of the bed.
The man squinches himself up against the back
of the woman, an arm crooks over her waist,
his hand touches sometimes her hand, sometimes her breast,
his penis settles along the groove between her buttocks,
falls into deep sleep, almost starts to snore.
If someone were to discover them this way,
him like the big, folded wings of her,
they might stay as they are, the way the woodcock,
believing herself safe in her camouflage, sometimes
sits still until a person stoops and reaches out to pet her—
then jumps six feet straight up and wherries off.
When the sun enters the room, he wakes and watches her.
Her hair lies loose, strewn across the pillow
as if it has been washed up, her lips are blubbed,
from the kissing, her profile is fierce,
like that of a figurehead seeing over
the rim of the world. She wakes.
They do not get up yet. It is not easy
to straighten out bodies that have been lying
all night in the same curve, like two paintbrushes
wintering in a coffee can of evaporated turpentine.
They hear the clangs of a church clock. Why only nine?
When they have been lying on this bed since before the earth began.

I sneaked out of the house after helping with the dishes.
I made my way to the deepest center of the woods and
climbed a young maple tree and gazed up into the deep-
ening sky above. I must have dozed off for a few minutes,
because quite suddenly the stars emerged in a blacker sky.
Although I did not know their names—in fact, I did not
even know they had names—I began to address them
quietly, for I never spoke with "full-throated ease" until
hidden by the cover of total darkness. A soft wind shook
the leaves around me. From my own hands I caught the
smell of earth and iron.

—Philip Levine

I would leave by the back door
and make my way to the woods, on paths
I thought were trails of the Wampanoags,
paths at that hour still woven over
with scaly, cobwebby stuff
that had dew under it and dew on top.
I pressed myself to a white oak
and climbed. On the way up gravity
seemed to start pulling me from above.
At the top of this somnolent fountaining
of trunk, boughs, branches, twigs, leaf-splashes,
all of it tinned with the industrial dust
of Pawtucket in Depression,
I gave my ape-cry.
I knew the oaks' sermon to us
has to do with their verticality,

and their muted budding and brilliant decay,
and their elasticity, and their suthering and creaking,
and now and then their dispersal at the top into birds.
But I knew it had to do even more
with this massive, stunting halt
and the 360° impetus to spill outward
and downward and hover above their twin
glooming open under the ground
—at Loon Lake I had seen this in visions.
Out of the hush and rustlings came
chirrups, whistlings, tremolos, hoots,
noises that seemed left poking up
after some immense subtraction.
Tok-tok-tok-tok, as from somebody
nailing upholstery, started up nearby:
the bird with a bloodmark on the back
of his head clung, cutting with
steady strokes his cave of wormwood.
On another tree, a smaller bird,
in gray rags, put her rump
to the sky and walked headfirst
down the trunk toward the earth
and the earth under the earth.
Drops of rain plopped into my hair.
I looked up and bigger drops tapped
my lips and cheeks. Unlike the cat,
who loves climbing but not coming down,
I came swinging and sliding down,
hanging by my knees on the last branch,

and, as if the tree were one bell
of an hourglass which had been taken up
and turned over while I was up in it
and just as I slid through set down hard,
I landed with a jounce. The drops
chuting earthward all around me
were bringing back a kind of time
that falls and does not fly.
The red-topped bird kept working in the rain.
I had seen my father stand most of a
day pushing and lifting
his handsaw. All hand tools, I thought,
were the trees' equals, working wood
no more easily than a woodpecker's auger.
I had not yet caught in the crosscut's
grunts and gasps the screams, in time
to come, of chainsaws, or in the steady,
drudging *hunhs!* of the ripsaw the howls
of supersaws clear-cutting the mountainsides,
or in the *har-har* and handshake
of the developer the loud bellowing
and hard squeeze of tree harvesters; I had not
conceived its own pulverized
pulp being ripped out in an arc at the foot
of every tree, I had not witnessed
the imperceptible budge, the dryadic pop,
the slow tilt and accelerating topple,
the dry splintering crash of tree
after tree like the end of history.

And yet—as I walked—a scrub pine brushed
dust off my pants, a birch branch knocked
debris of bark from my shirt, a leaf-clump
of a white cedar seemed to reach down and,
as if to preempt the work of the hairbrush
ready to harrow its spiky bristles across
my brain-skin in the morning at the front door
on my way to Sunday school, smoothed my sodden hair.

III

SHEFFIELD GHAZALS

THE BITING INSECTS

The biting insects don't like the blood of people who dread dying.
They prefer the blood of people who can imagine themselves entering
      other life-forms.
These are the ones the mosquito sings to in the dark and the deer fly
      orbits and studies with yellow eyes.
In the other animals the desire to die comes when existing wears out
      existence.
In us this desire can come too early, and we kill ourselves, or it may
      never come, and we have to be dragged away.
Not many are able to die well, not even Jesus going back to his father.
And yet dying gets done — and Eddie Jewell coming up the road with
      his tractor on a flatbed truck and seeing an owl lifting its wings
      as it alights on the ridgepole of this red house, Galway, will
      know that now it is you being accepted back into the family
      of mortals.

Some old people become more upset about human foibles than they
      did when they were younger—part of getting ready to leave.
For others, human idiocy becomes increasingly precious; they begin to
      see in it the state of mind we will have in heaven.
"What about heaven?" I said to Harold, who is ninety-four and lives
      in the VA Hospital in Tucson.
He said, "Memory is heaven."
The physicist emeritus tottering across the campus of Cal Tech
      through the hazy sunshine occasionally chuckles to himself.
Yet it has happened to many others, and to you, too, Galway—when
      illness, or unhappiness, or imagining the future wears an
      empty place inside us, the idea of paradise elsewhere quickly
      fills it.

COLLUSION OF ELEMENTS

On the riverbank *Narcissus poeticus* holds an ear trumpet toward the
    canoe apparitioning past.

Cosmos sulphureous flings back all its eyelashes and stares.

The canoe enacts the Archimedean collusion of elements: no matter
    how much weight you try to sink it with, the water as
    vigorously holds it up.

Up to a point.

Likewise, the more pressure the fuel exerts on the O-rings, the more
    securely they fit into their grooves and keep the fuel from
    escaping.

At certain temperatures.

Pain is inherently lonely.

Of all the varieties of pain, loneliness may be the most lonely.

The Queen Charlotte Islanders used the method of fire to hollow a
    canoe out of a single log.

If there are burn-throughs, a vessel could founder; if cold O-rings,
    blow up.

As for you, Galway, the more serious the burn-throughs and the
    looser the O-rings in their grooves, the greater the chance you
    could float or fly.

DRIVING WEST

A tractor-trailer carrying two dozen crushed automobiles overtakes a
        tractor-trailer carrying a dozen new.
Oil is a form of waiting.
The internal combustion engine converts the stasis of millennia into
        motion.
Cars howl on rain-wetted roads.
Airplanes rise through the downpour and throw us through the
        blue sky.
The idea of the airplane subverts earthly life.
Computers can deliver nuclear explosions to precisely anywhere
        on earth.
A lightning bolt is made entirely of error.
Erratic Mercurys and errant Cavaliers wander the highways.
A girl puts her head on a boy's shoulder; they are driving west.
The windshield wipers wipe, homesickness one way, wanderlust the
        other, back and forth.
This happened to your father and to you, Galway—sick to stay,
        longing to come up against the ends of the earth.

PASSING THE CEMETERY

Desire and act were a combination known as sin.

The noise of a fingernail on a blackboard frightened our bones.

Metacarpus, phalanges of thumb and fingers, distil phalanx of index,
ungual tuberosity, became visible when I put my hand to the
sun.

The stairwell on the way up to the dentist's smelled of the fire inside
teeth.

Passing the cemetery while eating a Clark bar, I wondered if the bones
of the dead at some point become brittle and crumbly.

A dog would gnaw its own skeleton down to nothing, if possible.

On Holytide Wednesday Catholic children came to school with
foreheads smudged, in penance beforehand, with what might
be left of their desires.

The old sermons on the evils of the flesh often caused portions of flesh
to lose feeling, sometimes to drop off.

If we press our frontal bones to the madrone, even in hottest July, the
chill of under the earth passes into us, making us shiver from
within.

A deathbed repentance intended to pluck out one bright terrible
thread could unravel a lifetime — and the lifetimes of people
left behind.

Fishes are the holy land of the sea.

In them spirit is flesh, flesh spirit, the brain simply a denser place in
the flesh.

The human brain is the brightest place on earth.

At death the body becomes foreign substance; a person who loved you
may wash and dress this one you believed for so long was you,
Galway, a few embrace the memory in it, but somewhere else
will know it and welcome it.

IV

PARKINSON'S DISEASE

While spoon-feeding him with one hand
she holds his hand with her other hand,
or rather lets it rest on top of his,
which is permanently clenched shut.
When he turns his head away, she reaches
around and puts in the spoonful blind.
He will not accept the next morsel
until he has completely chewed this one.
His bright squint tells her he finds
the shrimp she has just put in delicious.
Next to the voice and touch of those we love,
food may be our last pleasure on earth—
a man on death row takes his T-bone
in small bites and swishes each sip
of the jug wine around in his mouth,
tomorrow will be too late for them to jolt
this supper out of him. She strokes
his head very slowly, as if to cheer up
each separate discomfited hair sticking up
from its root in his stricken brain.
Standing behind him, she presses
her cheek to his, kisses his jowl,
and his eyes seem to stop seeing
and do nothing but emit light.
Could heaven be a time, after we are dead,
of remembering the knowledge
flesh had from flesh? The flesh
of his face is hard, perhaps
from years spent facing down others

until they fell back, and harder
from years of being himself faced down
and falling back in his turn, and harder still
from all the while frowning
and beaming and worrying and shouting
and probably letting go in rages.
His face softens into a kind
of quizzical wince, as if one
of the other animals were working at
getting the knack of the human smile.
When picking up a cookie he uses
both thumbtips to grip it
and push it against an index finger
to secure it so that he can lift it.
She takes him then to the bathroom,
where she lowers his pants and removes
the wet diaper and holds the spout of the bottle
to his old penis until he pisses all he can,
then puts on the fresh diaper and pulls up his pants.
When they come out, she is facing him,
walking backwards in front of him
and holding his hands, pulling him
when he stops, reminding him to step
when he forgets and starts to pitch forward.
She is leading her old father into the future
as far as they can go, and she is walking
him back into her childhood, where she stood
in bare feet on the toes of his shoes
and they foxtrotted on this same rug.

I watch them closely: she could be teaching him
the last steps that one day she may teach me.
At this moment, he glints and shines,
as if it will be only a small dislocation
for him to pass from this paradise into the next.

Talking with my beloved in New York
I stood at the outdoor public telephone
in Mexican sunlight, in my purple shirt.
Someone had called it a man/woman
shirt. The phrase irked me. But then
I remembered that Rainer Maria
Rilke, who until he was seven wore
dresses and had long yellow hair,
wrote that the girl he almost was
"made her bed in his ear" and "slept him the world."
I thought, OK this shirt will clothe the other in me.
As we fell into long-distance love talk
a squeaky chittering started up all around,
and every few seconds came a sudden loud
buzzing. I half expected to find
the insulation on the telephone line
laid open under the pressure of our talk
leaking low-frequency noises.
But a few yards away a dozen hummingbirds,
gorgets going drab or blazing
according as the sun struck them,
stood on their tail rudders in a circle
around my head, transfixed
by the flower-likeness of the shirt.
And perhaps also by a flush rising into my face,
for a word—one with a thick sound,
as if a porous vowel had sat soaking up
saliva while waiting to get spoken,
possibly the name of some flower

that hummingbirds love, perhaps
"honeysuckle" or "hollyhock"
or "phlox"—just then shocked me
with its suddenness, and this time
apparently did burst the insulation,
letting the word sound in the open
where all could hear, for these tiny, irascible,
nectar-addicted puritans jumped back
all at once, fast, as if the air gasped.

And now—after putting forward a "unified theory":
that the music resulting from any of the methods
of organizing English into rhythmic surges
can sound like the music resulting from any other,
being the music not of a method but of the language;
and after proposing that free verse is a variant
of formal verse, using unpredictably the acoustic
repetitions which formal verse employs regularly;
and after playing recordings of the gopher frog's
long line of glottal stops, sounding like rumblings
in an empty stomach, and the notes the hermit thrush
pipes one after another, then twangles together,
and the humpback whale's gasp-cries as it passes
out of the range of human perception of ecstasy,
and the wolf's howls, one, and then several,
and then all the pack joining in a polyphony
to whatever in the sunlit midnight sky
remains keeper of the axle the earth and
its clasped lovers turn upon and cry to;
and after playing recordings of an angakoq
chanting in Inuktitut of his trance-life as a nanuk,
a songman of Arnhem Land, Rahmani of Iran,
Neruda of Chile, Yeats, Thomas, Rukeyser,
to let the audience hear that our poems
are of the same order as those of the other animals
and are composed, like theirs, when we find ourselves
synchronized with the rhythms of the earth,
no matter where, in the city of Brno, which cried
its vowel too deep into the night to get it back,

or at Ma'alaea on Maui in Hawaii, still plumping
itself on the actual matter of pleasure there,
or here in St. Paul, Minnesota, where I lean
at a podium trying to draw my talk to a close,
or on Bleecker Street a time zone away in New York,
where only minutes ago my beloved may have
put down her book and drawn up her eiderdown
around herself and turned out the light—
now, causing me to garble a few words
and tangle my syntax, I imagine I can hear
her say my name into the slow waves
of the night and, faintly, being alone, sing.

RAPTURE

I can feel she has got out of bed.
That means it is seven A.M.
I have been lying with eyes shut,
thinking, or possibly dreaming,
of how she might look if, at breakfast,
I spoke about the hidden place in her
which, to me, is like a soprano's tremolo,
and right then, over toast and bramble jelly,
if such things are possible, she came.
I imagine she would show it while trying to conceal it.
I imagine her hair would fall about her face
and she would become apparently downcast,
as she does at a concert when she is moved.
The hypnopompic play passes, and I open my eyes
and there she is, next to the bed,
bending to a low drawer, picking over
various small smooth black, white,
and pink items of underwear. She bends
so low her back runs parallel to the earth,
but there is no sway in it, there is little burden, the day has hardly
        begun.
The two mounds of muscles for walking, leaping, lovemaking,
lift toward the east—what can I say?
Simile is useless; there is nothing like them on earth.
Her breasts fall full; the nipples
are deep pink in the glare shining up through the iron bars
of the gate under the earth where those who could not love
press, wanting to be born again.
I reach out and take her wrist

and she falls back into bed and at once starts unbuttoning my pajamas.
Later, when I open my eyes, there she is again,
rummaging in the same low drawer.
The clock shows eight. Hmmm.
With huge, silent effort of great,
mounded muscles the earth has been turning.
She takes a piece of silken cloth
from the drawer and stands up. Under the falls
of hair her face has become quiet and downcast,
as if she will be, all day among strangers,
looking down inside herself at our rapture.

THE ROAD ACROSS SKYE

> What is the "this"? The weasel's shriek, only that.
> —Lucien Stryk

Through the open window I can see the road
that climbs the flank of Sgurr na Connaich,
dips out of sight, reappears, twists
over the topmost ridge, and vanishes—
reminding me of the roads winding away
over rising land, which I cut out and pasted
into a childhood scrapbook, all of them
leading out of the mill town hidden
below the bottom edge of each picture.
A cow with draggled petticoat, her flat face
shoveling the way for the rest of her
through the soft-cornered geometry
of the trajectories of flies, approaches,
raises her head, half sticks it in the window,
and gives a low cry. Behind her,
on the wire of the fence, a coal tit
tweets—loudly, given his size. Behind him,
in the pasture, three lambs shove at each other
under the udder of a ewe, who now gives two of them
discouraging kicks and the third a welcoming bleat.
If I hadn't been watching I might have heard
only an ordinary rattle in a sheep's throat.
In the greengrocer's on Wednesday a poster
announced LIFE HAS MEANING and if we tune in
to the wireless next Thursday, Friday, and Saturday

Billy Graham will tell us what it is.
From the next room my beloved calls,
in high notes, as from a treetop, "Some *tea?*"
and my head, fallen forward
at the thought of Billy Graham, pops up,
the way a weasel sticks his head out of his hole
at the vibration of footsteps. The dying Zen master
Daibei, hearing a weasel shriek, sat down
and composed his unrenounceable *jisei*—
"I am one with this, this only," it begins—
and told his disciples to remember to point out,
when they recited it, that the "this"
was the shriek, only that, and toppled over. "Yes,"
I call back. "With a little honey. And your company."
A baby named Hunter dribbles milk down his chin,
lies back, holds his left arm out straight
as if gripping the bow and his right bent over
the top of his head as if drawing the string,
and sleeps, in the night sky, all over the half-world,
on Thursday. On Friday and Saturday, *taisches,*
spirits of people who are about to die, wander the fields,
composing their farewells; those could be two,
there, perched on either side of the tit,
passing their last afternoon as feathery puffs
with quick hearts, to make musical *jisei.*
What sets the road climbing across Skye
apart from the roads in the scrapbook
is that, as it goes, it leaves me content to be
left here with all this. I think I might yet

get conscripted into the choir of the coal tit,
the cow, the ewe, the lambs, the weasel, Daibei,
the *taisches,* even the Reverend Billy, and especially
she who just cried to me from a treetop,
if I could sing all this to her without ceasing
so that it will not turn into all that.

V

LACKAWANNA

Possibly a child is not damaged immediately
but only after some time has passed.
When the parent who sits on the edge
of the bed leans over and moves an elbow
or a forearm or a hand across the place
where the child's torso divides into legs
at last gets up and goes to the door and turns
and says in an ordinary voice, "Good night,"
then in exactly eight minutes a train
in the freight yards on the other side of town
howls, its boxcar loaded up, its doors
rusted shut, its wheels clacking
over the tracks   *lacka   wanna   lacka.*
It may be that the past has the absolute force
of the law that visits parent upon child
unto the third or fourth generation, and the implacability
of vectors, which fix the way a thing
goes reeling according to where it was touched.
What is called spirit may be the exhaust-light
of toil of the kind a person goes through
years later to take any unretractable step
out of that room, even a step no longer
than a platinum-iridium bar in a vault in Paris,
and flesh the need afterwards to find
the nearest brasserie and mark with both elbows
on the zinc bar the start and the finish.
Never mind. The universe is expanding.
Soon they won't know where to look to find you.
There will be even more room when the sun dies.

It will be eight minutes before we know it is dead.
Plenty of time for the ordinary human acts
that will constitute our final mayhem.
In the case of a house there may be less room
when the principal occupants die, especially
if they refuse to leave and keep on growing.
Then in a few years the immaterial bulk
of one of them padding up from the dark
basement can make the stairs shriek
and the sleeper sit up, pivot out of bed, knock
an arm on the dresser, stand there shaking
while the little bones inside the elbow cackle.
The mind can start rippling again at any time
if what was thrown in was large, and thrown in early.
When the frequency of waves increases,
so does the energy. If pressure builds up,
someone could die from it. If they had been
able to talk with him, find out what he was going through,
the children think it would not have been him.
Inquiring into the situation of a thing
may alter the comportment, size, or shape of it.
The female nurse's elbow, for instance,
bumping a penis, could raise it up,
or the male doctor's hand, picking it up
and letting it drop a couple of times for
unexplained medical reasons, could slacken it.
Or vice versa. And the arm passing across it,
like Ockham's razor grabbed off God's chin
eight minutes before the train howls,

could simplify it nearly out of existence.
Is it possible, even, that Werner Heisenberg,
boy genius, hit on his idea in eight minutes?
The train sounds its horn and clickets over
the tracks   *lacka   wanna*   shaking up
a lot of bones trying to lie unnoticed
in the cemeteries. It stops to let off
passengers in a town, as the overturned grail
of copper and tin, lathed and fettled off
to secure its pure minor tierce, booms out
from the sanctus-turret those bulging notes
which, having been heard in childhood,
seem to this day to come from heaven.
So in memory, an elbow, which is without flesh,
touching a penis, which is without bone,
can restart the shock waves of being the one chosen,
even in shame, in a childhood of being left out.
But no one gets off. And a hand
apports in the center of a room suddenly
become empty, which the child has to fill
with something, with anything, with the ether
the Newtonian physicists manufactured
to make good the vacuums in the universe
or the nothing the God of the beginning
suctioned up off the uninhabited earth
and held all this time and now must exhale
back down, making it hard, for some, to breathe.
The hand suspended in the room still has
a look of divinity; every so often

it makes sweet sounds—music can't help it; like maggots
it springs up anywhere. The umbilical string
rubs across the brain, making it
do what it can, sing.

Parmenides: Would you feel, Socrates, that mud or hair or that matter that is even more worthless and vile has an idea which is distinct from the thing we can see and touch?

Socrates: Certainly not. Things of that kind are exactly as they appear. Though sometimes I become troubled and think that everything must have an idea. But the moment I think this, I run from the thought, in fear that I will fall into a bottomless pit of nonsense and perish.
—Plato

Jesus ate and drank but did not defecate.
—Valentinus

The trees and the herbs of the earth bring forth boughs, leaves, flowers, and fruits. A man brings forth nits, lice, and tapeworms. They distill and pour out oil, wine, and balms, and a man makes excrements of spittle, piss, and shit. They smell and breathe all sweetness, whereas man belches, breaks wind, and stinks.
—Innocent III

A man is, first, fetid sperm, then a sack of excrement, then food for worms.
—Saint Bernard

And þarfor says Saynt Bernard right:
Si diligenter cansideres quid per os,
quid per nares, ceterosque meatus
corporis egreditur, vilius sterquilinium
nunquam vidisti.
"If þow wille," he says, "ententyfly se,

And by-hald what comes fra þe
What thurgh mouthe, what thurgh nese, commonly,
And thurgh other overtes of his body,
A fouler myddyng saw þow never nane,"
Þan a man es, with flesche and bane.

— Richard Rolle of Hampole

O wombe! O bely! O stynkyng cod,
Fulfilled of dong and of corrupcioun!
At either end of thee foul is the soun.

— Chaucer's Pardoner

Through the pores there is an incessant oozing and
trickling as from a kettle of fat. The body is always
discharging matter, like a ripe boil, through its nine
orifices. Matter is secreted from the eyes, wax from the
ears, snot from the nostrils, food, bile, phlegm, and
blood from the mouth, shit and piss from the two lower
orifices, and from the ninety-nine thousand pores, a
foul sweat that attracts flies and other insects.

— Buddhaghosa

Blessed are you, Adonai, Eloheinu, King of the World,
who has formed the human body in wisdom and cre-
ated in it cavities and orifices. It is well known before
your seat of glory that if any of these be opened or any
of these be blocked, it is impossible to stand before you,
blessed Adonai, physician to all flesh, wondrous maker.

— *Shacharit*

Let us also consider the gifts of the belly and hind end,
how necessary they be, without which we cannot live.

A man or woman may live without eyes, ears, hands, feet, etc.; but (*salva reverentia*) without the hind end no human creature can survive; so great and necessary is the use and profit of this one part, that to it belongeth the preservation of human existence. Therefore St. Paul saith well (1 Cor. xii), "Those parts of the body that we think less honorable we clothe with greater honor, and our less respectable parts are treated with greater respect."

—Martin Luther

All attitudes, all the shapeliness, all the belongings of
     my or your body or of any one's body, male or
     female,
The lung-sponges, the stomach-sac, the bowels sweet
     and clean...
O I think now these are not the parts and poems of the
     body only but of the soul,
O I think these are the soul!

—Walt Whitman

I gathered all my courage, as though I were about to leap forthwith into hell-fire, and let the thought come. I saw before me the cathedral, the blue sky. God sits on His golden throne, high above the world—and from under the throne an enormous turd falls upon the sparkling new roof, shatters it, and breaks the walls of the cathedral asunder....Why did God befoul His cathedral? That, for me, was a terrible thought. But then came the dim understanding that God could be

something terrible. I had experienced a dark and terri-
ble secret. It overshadowed my whole life, and I became
deeply pensive.

—C. G. Jung

Often we forget, and imagine we're immortal.
If the gods don't shit, why must we?
And we would feel distinctly less like animals
if only we could sever the chain of linked turds
tying us to some hole in the ground—
the cesspool Dante used as his model for hell
or the pit Martin Luther squatted over,
after six days of clogged bowels, while
receiving the doctrine of justification by faith,
an epiphany that came with a stink
of the kind Swift's alter ego met on lifting
the lid of his beloved's chamber pot
(he was slow to believe it): "Oh Celia, Celia,
Celia shits!" But think, last night
you took what you liked from a carrot,
today you give back the rest.
For hours each day the child Genet
roosted in the silken peace of the outhouse,
a confessional where we bare our intimate parts,
feeding his imagination on the odor and darkness.
For myself, it was many years before I could
get near the poetry section in a bookstore
or PS3521 in library stacks
without a sudden urge to shit,

I don't know why, unless envy, or emulation,
a need, like a coyote's or hyena's,
to set down my identity in scat.
The white-tailed deer stops and solfs her
quarter notes the size and color
of niçoise olives onto the snow. The canary
sands off the hull with her gizzard
and sleets it to the cage floor, trilling
the entire kernel of the seed into song.
My father grunted — I heard him —
on the horseshoe of the toilet seat;
I pictured one of the *noctis equii*
kicking him in the rear end, knocking a lump
out of him, into the still water, causing
its surface, thinner than brow skin, to worry all over.
Thirty-five thousand feet up a fountain pen sheisses
into a shirt pocket a purplish black gush that can now
never become one of the great elemental words —
*fire   night   wind   shit.**

---

*Shit: At the present time an indecent word,
          which the newspapers that were enamored
          of the smart weapons of the Gulf War,
          which kill so far away you could never
          hear the screams or see the blood,
          won't print, despite a lineage going back
          to the Indo-European, from *skheid,*
          to shed, to drop, and its wide lead
          over the other expletives in frequency
          of use, even the divine three,
          God, Christ, and fuck.

Coming home, she said, "Yes, there's
the bag, and the fuss, and the mess.
But what I hate most is that I'll never
sit down ever again and take a good shit."
After five years of captivity the ex-hostage said,
"Nobody says it, but one of the blessings
of being free is going to the bathroom when you want."
A horsebun turns golden in the September sun,
a cowflap in a pasture wrinkles pinkish.
On the kitchen shelf a fieldmouse lays its
turds at the foot of a box of whole-grout oats.
The black bear who swatted down the apples
from the lower branches began before first light
expelling foot-long cylinders of apple-chompings
—some apple nectar removed, some bear nectar added—
which could almost be served up in a restaurant
in Lyons or Paris as Compote de Pommes des Dieux.
Well, we eat shit anyway. Consider
andouilles and *boudins noirs.*
And don't *boeuf,* whom we castrate and strip
of all function except to divide grass
into shit and flesh that soon will be mostly shit,
look like lumps skheided into the field
by a something else? Of course, as cummings'
Olaf, "whose warmest heart recoiled at war,"
declared, "there is some s. I will not eat."
Like the s. of having to print it as *s.*
Or of imagining we are a people who don't die,
who come out of the sky like gods and drop

not shit but bombs on people who shit.
We don't know what life is, but we know
all who live on earth eat, sleep, mate, work,
shit, and die. Let us remember this is our home
and that we have become, we mad ones, its keepers.
Let us sit bent forward slightly, and be opened a moment,
as earth's holy matter passes through us.

FLIES

Walt Whitman noticed a group of them
suspended near his writing table at lunchtime;
at sunset he looked up and there they still were,
"balancing in the air in the centre of the room, darting athwart, up and
      down, casting swift shadows in specks on the opposite wall
      where the shine is."
When a person sits concentrating hard,
flies often collect in one spot, in a little bunch,
not far from the brain, and fly through each other.
The next day you can see them in a shaft
of sunlight in the barn, going over an intricacy.
Sometimes they alight on my writing-fingers
as I form letters that look like drawings of them,
or sit on the typewriter watching the keys hit,
perhaps with some of the alert misapprehension
of my mother, when I was in high school,
at the sporadic clacking coming from my room.
Karl Shapiro addressed a fly:
"O hideous little bat, the size of snot!"
Yesterday I killed a fly that had been trying
to crawl up a nostril and usurp a snot's niche.
On being swatted, it jettisoned itself
into my cup of coffee. When I swat and miss,
the fly sometimes flies to the fly swatter,
getting out of striking range by going deeper
inside it, like a child hugging the person who has just
struck her. Or it might alight on my head.
Miroslav Holub says that at the battle of Crécy a fly

                    alighted
        on the blue tongue
        of the Duke of Clervaux.

When Emily Dickinson's dying person dies, a fly's
"blue – uncertain – stumbling Buzz" goes with her
as far as it can go. If you fire the stoves
in a closed-up house in the fall, the cluster flies,
looking groggy, will creep from their chinks
and sleeping-holes, out of seeming death.
Soon, if the sun is out, hundreds will appear,
as if being born right there on the window glass.
When so many vibrate together, the murmur
Christopher Smart called the "honey of the air"
becomes a howl. Seiki observes in himself
what is true of me too:

        Once I kill
        A fly I find I
        Want to massacre them all.

Then Antonio Machado cries *But…but…they*

                have rested
        upon the enchanted toy
        upon the large closed book,
        upon the love letter,
        upon the stiffened eyelids
        of the dead.

John Clare, who came like the Baptist to prepare us
for the teachings of Darwin, tells us flies
"look like things of the mind or fairies, and seemed pleased or dull

as the weather permits in many clean cottages, and genteel
houses, they are allowed every liberty to creep, fly or do as they
like, and seldom or ever do wrong, in fact they are the small or
dwarfish portion of our own family."
James K. Baxter said New Zealand flies regard him as their *whenua*,
which in Maori means both placenta and land.
In the year of Clare's birth, William Blake asks:

Am not I
A fly like thee?
Or art not thou
A man like me?

He could not have known the tsetse spits into its bite
the trypanosome, which releases into us
a lifetime supply of sleep, even some extra,
or that the flashy, green, meat-eating botfly
needs flesh to bury its eggs in, living flesh will do,
or that his diminutive cousin, that fly
walking on the lips of his baby, scatters manure
behind him as copiously as the god Sterquilius.
Martin Luther said, "I am a bitter enemy to flies. When I open a book
for the first time, flies land on it at once, with their hind ends,
and nose around, as if they would say, 'Here we will squat, and
besmirch this book with our excrement.'"
The wanton among us, who kill flies for our sport,
like to hear of the evil flies do. Then we swat
with more pleasure, as if we did God's work.
"Is this thy play?" Edward Taylor cries. "For why?"
I think I have a fly inside me.

It drones through me,
at three A.M., looking for what stinks,
the more stinking the better, a filth heap
old or new, some regret, or guilt, or humiliation,
and finds it, and feeds, waking me,
and I live it again. Then, with an effort
of will feeble enough if compared with my mother's
when I arrived almost too late at her deathbed
and she broke back through her last coma and spoke,
I swing at it, and it jumps up and swerves away.
I do not think this fly will ever go.
It feels like part of me, and it might not leave
until I rattle out a regret
sufficient to the cause and close the account.
Then it might come out and, if the stove is lit
and the autumn sun bright, fly to the window
above the table, or, if the day is gloomy,
crawl up my upper lip and enter
that nostril at last. So I swat,
flailing at the window without aiming,
until the windowsill, and the big, open
Webster's First, and the desk and part of the floor
are speckled with their paltry remains,
strewn thick as the human dead in the Great War.
One of them rights itself, and walks,
and seems to feel OK, and flies.
My father righted himself out of the muck
where many thousands of dead
stuck out their blue tongues. The Preacher says,

"Dead flies cause the ointment of the apothecary to send forth a
          stinking savour."
Would that muck were an ointment a chthonic
apothecary oozes up in the earth's devastated places.
But no one who rights himself out of it
and walks and feels OK
is OK.
He knows something, and wants to keep others
from smelling it on him and knowing that he is
the fly in the ointment, wherever he flies.
As the treetops' shadow climbs the window
the flies creep up just ahead of it.
They often collide, and seem troubled and confused,
as though they came here for something
and have forgotten what, and keep looking anyway,
like my father, on coming to America.
When a fly stands motionless on a window,
I wonder if it is looking through the bottom
facets of its eye at the outdoors.
Federico García Lorca said that when
a fly buzzes inside a window,

> I think of people
> in chains.
> And I let it go free.

A fly may not always want to go free,
though the radiant heat through the barrier of glass
may let it imagine that it does. In this
it would be like my mother, in her ardor

for poetry, before she found out
that poetry was what I was up to in my life
—though not in her craving for love in her own life.
When she looked with her blue eye I am sure
it seemed wild and fiery out there and she knew she must go.
I find it hard to imagine that she did not,
at some point, with her big, walker's feet, tread hard
and break through. More than once I felt
a draft of icy air. But my sisters say no.

THE STRIPED SNAKE AND THE GOLDFINCH

I

When I pick up the corner of the sheet of black
plastic spread over last year's potato patch,
a striped snake two feet long lifts her head.
When I take her by the back of the neck, she writhes,
seeking purchase so she can throw herself and bite,
her tongue zzzing like an arc welder rumpling out
a brass bandage, rough as the gossamers snakes
slough on mountain paths, which crested flycatchers
snatch up and weave into their nests to hex cowbirds.
Trying to slide away, she goes through one of my hands
and finds the other waiting to draw her back.
Up on my shoulder, she drags herself across my nape,
turns, drags herself back again across my Adam's apple,
making me think of one of those high-limb rope saws
you work from the ground by pulling alternately
on the two control cords, sawing off my head.
Now she crawls over me more slowly and drapes herself,
and I can feel what seems her pleasure, and
I am happy to be her somewhat living warm object.
Sliding halfway off my hand, she holds herself
with forepart pulled down like a wand of applewood
straining toward water under the black soil
where the worms rumba, streams to the ground
like a spirit going from me, wriggles over
to the black plastic, pauses, and slides under.

2

Stepping into the woods, I remember going
alone into Seekonk Woods when I was ten,
sometimes wondering: Who would I be?
Would I find work I could do? Could I love,
or be loved? Was being, for me, even possible?
Looking back, I have to squint, to see those days
which I spent as if walking at night in a village
high in the Alps, when the lights in the valley
seem farther away than the stars, passing houses
where a man and a woman lie asleep
in one room, and children sleep in another,
and in a courtyard a dog, hearing someone
unfamiliar walking at the wrong hour, wakes—
someone smoking a cigarette, like the cigarette my father
dragged on, as he sat in mud, its periodic glow
proof he existed, while shells shrieked overhead
and exploded in other trenches, the trench
where his brother David blew up many times
in imagination, wrote one letter to his mother
praying he might live to come home, blew up
into parts some of which may have got mixed up
with some of someone else's — and barks, *proof,*
and again, double-checking, *proof proof,* and then,
hearing no one, goes back to sleep, and the village
snow creaks as if the press of nightwalking hurt it.

3

How much do I have left of the loyalty to earth,
which human shame, and dislike of our own lives,
and others' deaths that take part of us with them,
wear out of us, as we go toward that moment
when we find out how we die: clinging and pleading,
or secretly relieved that it is all over,
or despising ourselves, knowing that death
is a punishment we deserve, or like an old dog,
off his feed, who suddenly is ravenous,
and eats the bowl clean, and the next day is a carcass.
There is an unfillableness in us — in some of us,
a longing for that blue-shaded black night
where the beloved dead, and all those others
who suffered and sang and were not defeated—
the one who hushed them by singing "Going Home"
when they lynched him on Bald Mountain,
the klezmer violinists who pressed bows
across strings until eyes, by near-starvation
enlarged, grew wet and sparkled — have gone.
Yet I know more than ever that here is the true place,
here where we sit together, out of the wind,
with a loaf of country bread, and tomatoes still warm
from the distant sun, and wine in glasses that are,
one for each of us, the upper bell of the glass
that will hold the last hour we have to live.

4

Coming out of the woods I cross the field,
check the black plastic — nobody — and go up
to the house. Inside there is a flurry of clicks —
a goldfinch, who must have flown in the open door
on seeing sky in the window in the opposite wall,
flies at window glass, beak and talons hitting
it like a telegraph key sending · · · – – – · · ·
Holding a towel to the glass, I bunch it around the bird,
take the bundle to the door, reach in
and draw the soft-surfaced, distinct body
into the brilliant sunshine. He looks at me, his eye guarded,
unforthcoming, with the blankness of an old person
on a gurney staring at corridor ceilings
on the way to surgery. Perhaps also with defiance.
I search it for signs of eros — before long
a bird can start courting us, if we have rescued it,
put splints on a leg or wing, eyedroppered it sugary water,
deposited mealworms and pieces of fruit
down its throat, surrounded it in a warm hand
that brings back an embryo-memory of the hot,
featherless brood patch which darkened upon the egg,
like the lead aprons the good dentists Landa
and Silloway have spread, huge and heavy, on me,
or the tongue of God pressed to a body just
before giving it that vast lick from head to tail.

5

When I open my hand, wherever I had touched him
looks corroded; wherever I had not shines
his original lemon yellow. He sits a moment,
as if half-limed. But, his *odorat* undeveloped,
unresponsive to the 2-methyl-3-hexanoic
which the lipophilic diptheroids of my hand
release through the wrinkles cross-stitching
each other down the heart line, he flies,
dipping and lifting like a needle basting a hem,
disappears into the intertangled branches of the birches
Inés and I planted in the spring of our marriage
six hundred and thirteen years ago, if you go
by the affection-rings and the weariness-rings
inside the trunk when the magician saws it through,
and opens it, and finds each of you cut in half,
separated from yourself at the waist. There he is,
in a birch top, its crown. Meanwhile the snake
may have crawled up my spine to sit in my mouth
and utter an unsteady flame. I think I will fly
for a while now in the world that exists
the height of the human head above the ground.
A boy who stood in Seekonk Woods might like
living out this life; he might even count it a worthy destiny
to pass, in rhythmic flight, with *zzzing* tongue,
through this heaven, some moments, on the way to death.

Bending over her bed, I saw the smile
I must have seen when I looked up from the crib.
Knowing death comes, imagining it, smelling it,
may be a fair price for consciousness.
But looking at my sister lying there, I wished
she could have been snatched up from behind
to die by surprise, without ever knowing about death.
Too late. Wendy said, "I am in three parts.
Here on the left is red. That is pain.
On the right is yellow. That is exhaustion.
The rest is white. I don't know yet what white is."
For most people, one day everything is OK.
The next, the limbic node catches fire. The day after,
the malleus in one ear starts missing the incus.
Then the arthritic opposable thumb no longer opposes
whoever screwed the top onto the jam jar.
Then the coraco-humeral ligament frizzles apart,
the liver speckles, the kidneys dent,
two toes lose their souls. Of course,
before things get worse, a person could run.
I could take off right now, climb the pure forms
that surmount time and death, follow a line
drawn along Avenue D, make a 90° turn right on 8th Street,
90° left on C, right on 7th, left on B, then cross
to Sixth Avenue, catch the A train to Nassau,
the station where the A pulls up beside the Z,
get off and hop on the Z and hurtle under the river
and rise on Euclid under the stars and taste,
with a woman, in perfectly circular kisses,

the actual honey of paradise.
Then, as if Wendy suddenly understood
this flaw in me, that I could die
still wanting what is not to be had here, drink
and drink and yet have most of my thirst
intact for the water table, she opened her eyes.
"I want you to know I'm not afraid of dying,"
she said. "I only wish it didn't take so long."
Seeing her look so young and begin to die
all on her own, I wanted to whisk her off.
Quickly she said, "Let's go home." From outside
in the driveway came the gargling noise
of a starter motor, and a low steady rumbling, as if
my car had turned itself on and was warming up the engine.
She said this as if we had gone over to visit
a friend, to sign our names on the plaster cast
on her leg, broken on the swing in our backyard,
and some awful indoor game had gone wrong,
and Wendy had turned to me and said, "Let's go home."
She had closed her eyes. She looked entirely white.
Her hair had been white for years; in her illness
her skin was as if powdered with twice-bleached flour;
now her lips seemed to have given up their blood.
Color flashed only when she opened her eyes.
Snow will come down next winter, in the woods;
the fallen trees will have that flesh on their bones.
When the eye of the woods opens, a bluejay shuttles.
Outside, suddenly, all was quiet, and
I realized my car had shut off its engine.

And now she felt hot to the touch, as if
an almost immaterial fat were still clinging,
like a lining, to the inside of her skin,
burning. There was a looseness to her flesh.
A translucency came into it, as had happened
with our mother when she was about to die.
At last a spot of rosiness showed in each cheek:
blushes, perhaps, at a joy she had kept from us,
from somewhere in her life, perhaps two mouths,
hers and a beloved's, near each other, like roses
sticking out of a bottle of invisible water.
She was losing the half-given, half-learned
art of speech, and it became a struggle for her
to find the words, to form them, to position them,
and then quickly utter them. After much effort
she said to me, "Now is when the point of the story changes."
After that, one eye at a time, the left listened,
and drifted, the right focused, gleamed
meanings at me, drifted. Stalwart,
the halves of the brain, especially the right.
Now, as they ratchet the box holding
her body into the earth, I hear her voice,
calling back across the region she passes through,
in prolonged, even notes, which swell and diminish,
a far landscape I seem to see as if from above,
much light, much darkness, tumbling clouds,
sounding back to us from its farthest edge.
Now her voice comes from under the horizon,
and now it grows faint, and now I cannot hear it.

811.54   Kinnell, Galway,
KIN   1927-

        Imperfect thirst.

                              59022

$19.95

DATE			
JAN - 6 1995			
JUL 1 0 1995			